C H I E M I

KARMA BANK *to*

Following by Listening

For more information about Chiemi, go to

www.ChiemiMusic.com

ISBN 978-1-66781-319-6 (Print)

ISBN 978-1-66781-320-2 (eBook)

This is dedicated to those who listen
and have listened to my songs, tunes,
ditties and written meanderings for years,
providing invaluable feedback, suggestions,
support and encouragement along the way.
I am ever grateful to you.

Sometimes I feel like creating is following by listening, trying not to get in the way, and reflecting things back because they are bigger than you, just (hopefully) adding your own insight so that they can go back out into the world. These are some of the things I've heard recently and in the past few years. I was introduced to this sort of listening in 2019, when someone suggested to me that experiences of grace and acts of generosity might be viewed as coins that we put in the karma bank.

Chiemi

OCTOBER 2021

Table of Contents

1. Collection From the Karma Bank

These are tales, tides and tinkling lights – tunes telling stories of warmth and sun, city and sand, paths that lead, and the coins we can keep in the Karma Bank. Spirit's been bypassed for sorrow, dreaming of a better tomorrow …

1. When People Matter
2. Stories We Tell Ourselves
3. Other Spectral Flames
4. See Our Déjà vu
5. Evacuation Day
6. Nuance (Preserve the Mystery)
7. Seasons Bypassed Altogether
8. Coins in the Karma Bank
9. Taking a Taste
10. Inside Dancing Feet

When People Matter ⤿⤾ SEPTEMBER 28, 29, 30 / 2020

And you want to catch it, (to) whisper it,
Faint like fireflies.
Because the tide can, come up to the treetops,
And buildings dissolve in sand.
You've something left in, the soundlessness,
Amber surge, (sweet) taste of brine.

People who matter, haunt us in moments,
Stay with us, seep words in our days,
Where memory and motion, aren't evenly weighted,
People who matter take all.

Outside the porthole, dusk softens tree points,
Like turtles, we're hidden and exposed.
All at once, we're just people,
Blue tinge yields to dawn.

(Some) people surprise, link things other say,
Should not be connected,
Shape perception, for the future,
Dancers with no tune, just beat.

A ball thrown, wants to be caught,
So it won't fall forever …
You can live in this thin crust,
Never see the underground river …

Winter evening, grey mirror pavement
I reach to grasp your missive.
Flashing color, for my eye to interpret,
Dark scribble in a pale sky.

A saga of blessing
Green long since, burned away
By the sun on the sea
Fish darkening water
Sky shimmers, fractured light ...

Your same self
Can be elsewhere, sometimes ...
Continue those silent conversations
Leaving rain in the voice ...
Letting night birds drop from above ...

> Yet horses are running ... deep under the earth
> And we are so aware ... no need for complete sentences.
> Your can hear the fighting breeze ... and the splash of water
> hitting ground ...
> How laughter sounds in open air ∼

Storms blow through us
Time measured in meaning
Displacing air in a room ...
What you don't realize you say ...
Stories we show to one another ...

> Do I feel a ghost, like a voice from an empty campfire?
> Sometimes what seems like smoke, turns out to be rain ...
> Do I hear some notes, like a line from an unsung lullaby
> Something that looks like smoke, could always be rain ... ∼

Black water at night
Collects on the shore path
Light pieces, brilliant and scattered ...
(You) shield your eyes, squinting to see ...
Stories we tell ourselves ...

Other Spectral Flames ⟿ MAY 2020

Fleeting impressions, expressions of you
In a bird's eye, a continuing reflection, caught in limbo …
Maybe moving forward or away … to a better place, anyway … anyway …

In another world, just beyond sight
A seascape bleeding, a sunset blaze
Violent pink streaked with orange …
Doused in the ocean, burning the sky … burning the sky …

We feel dizzy and sometimes fall
But keep walking where sorrow and joy intersect …
In the strings of an instrument, coloring vast distance …
Where pipe dreams can continue … continue …

My ship on the horizon's suspended
Between air and water aflame
Confused visions captured
In a shifting boat, fading into morning … into morning …

Was there an explosion?
Dust settles, forms necklaces … outlining what remains
The fan of memory, with its folds
Hiding the truth, when our endings don't belong … don't belong …

See Our Déjà Vu

Names change, depending on
who is speaking.
We are all books,
But with different histories …
Memories not exploring the past,
But its theatre …

> It's like waking up in a dream,
> (To) go straight to the shore,
> (Just) footsteps away,
> Down a mountain of rock,
> And in another dream, in another dream …

The birth of anything,
Looks like a wound,
But nothing is born,
Without bleeding, some pain …
Growth to explore the future,
And its theatre …

> Déjà vu's not real,
> It only exists in your mind.
> Like magic, you feel,
> Something, not real.
> Something not real,
> Just like something here …

People define
one another like colors.
There's no pure, blue, red or yellow,
Just the present uncertainty,
The good kind, in theatre …

EVACUATION DAY IN BOSTON IS REMEMBERED AS THE DAY WHEN THE BRITS LEFT. IN 2020, IT WAS THE DAY WHEN COVID BECAME REAL AND HAD EFFECT, CAUSING THE CITY TO BE VACATED ... HAWAII BEACHES TO BE VACATED ... THE BEGINNING OF EVERYTHING COMING TO A HALT. WE'LL NEVER BE THE SAME.

Evacuation Day ∼ MARCH 17 / 2020

It's a song too familiar, to need an author
Looking thru the lens, of what we know now …
Not the people we were, but the people we are …
Not the people we were, but the people we are …
     We are all quarantined, or about to be …
     Being in, kept in … Being with, how strange, or about to be …
What are silent conversations?
What comes of them?
Lots of strands, like seaweed … living intersections
Maybe they follow, coalesce … converge, then change …
Re-emerge again.

You run and run, turn into smoke,
Float and float, drawn to beauty …
A sun formed of crushed stars …
A wave's kiss slaps the shore …
Flowers with roots, bound to earth.
The dizzing tide pulls away from your feet,
Your fingers in the sand …
Blown by the wind …
Across streets, under doors …
Makes us want to listen, makes us want to hear …
Makes us want to listen, makes us want to be near …

Nuance (Preserve the Mystery)

Can your story sing?
Words left over from another time … a special time …
Within walls, with people like you, with you …

Preserve the mystery … it has a purpose …
Sometimes, keeping layers …
All that nuance … makes beauty …
Makes beauty …

Sharing stories … memories …
To build a new future … from the one before …
We were all made to meet … and see in a new color …

Preserve the mystery …

Another range … an octave between …
Where we could touch … and where we need to go …
The space in between … imagine that place …

Are there memories locked inside …
A house with no doors …

Shadows falling; falling shadows …
Across the floor …
What is done … undone …
Ashy twilight …

Preserve the mystery … it has a purpose …
Sometimes, keeping layers …
All that nuance … makes beauty …
Makes beauty …

Seasons Bypassed Altogether

Two friends, walk on rocks …
What do they talk about?
Streams running into pools …
What do they talk about?
Piano strains from a pocket …
What do they talk about?
A device that carries, creating backdrop …
What do they talk about?

       Visions don't come with explanations …
       They are still yellow, disappearing …
       Like an eclipse, June twilight …
       Seasons bypassed altogether …
       Seasons bypassed altogether …

See the white moon sliver …
A trick, some shadow …
Are colors revealed?
What do they talk about?

Words are streams, meandering lines …
What do they talk about?
Turning and shaping memory …
The ghost of who you used to be …

SOMETIMES YOU MAY JUST NEED TO REFLECT ...
DREAMING OF A BETTER TOMORROW ...

Coins in the Karma Bank ∿➥ MARCH 2019

What if the crystals piled up and stuck,
Despite the wind.
Expressions fade, but remain as gems …

Kind acts, before a sinking ship …
Mutual sharing, is a natural gift.
Digits on hold, feel my nails …
Coins in the karma bank …
Coins in the karma bank.

I see a flag and stairs …
Buildings in the sun and snow …
Pills through a window …

Kind acts, before a sinking ship …

Does my rosary matter …
My spirit's been bypassed for sorrow …
Dreaming of a better tomorrow …
Dreaming of a better tomorrow …

Kind acts, before a sinking ship …

Taking a Taste

Writing a work that could end at any moment.
Not just the now, different versions of validity …
To go on living, love is like grace
If it fades, warm memory still enfolds
Even if flowers, had no chance to grow,
Sun rays, no place to fall …

(But) I thought I saw
Pools and streams
With tender trees by logs drowned
Rising up from a lake like mystery
Deep and dark, beauty a given …

Shadows of wasps on the windowsill
Black against glare, they move towards the light
Unable to reach it, following each other …
No way to escape, they still face outside,
Light is all they know

    You may see a stranger, and see a soul
    Like a flame, there's no turning away …
    You may feel air, moving and alive
    Laced with lime, marshy tang on your face …

The ornery have no easy answers
No plain meanings, just hidden patterns.
Mystical modes can plumb their wrought paths.
With good self-doubt, your world becomes altered …
Let go of your view, it may no longer be true
A taste can change your way.

PHOTO BY KEN BERNSTEIN

Inside Dancing Feet ⌇⌐ NOVEMBER 27- 29 / 2020

When you get inside of it, consumed by the wind,
Breathing a melody, you don't understand.
Another place to see and reach …

When you're out of body, you always come down,
Your spirit needs dancing feet, moving without words …

> What is simple, yet beautiful from attention,
> (Like) finding a secret room in your house.
> Time is not endless, try to hold it in your hands …
> And it will always slip away. [Chorus]

> Sky lying everywhere, hot blue above,
> Long grass, rippled; urban whispers too,
> Concrete with spider cracks, street whir & café glass,
> Birds who see it from a distance.

When you dream, you sail through grass,
No boat, no pole, no black water …
When you dream, you move like a heron,
Wings beating on, no hard landing. [Chorus]

> You can be still, like a cat who draws you in,
> Never giving too much away …
> But it's the eyes, that let you inside,
> So you can see the dancing feet.

ii. Still Wide Awake in the Now

Evocative songs about living in this time, seeking serenity, and appreciating what we have.

1. Where There Are Sparks
2. Other Openings
3. Unled Lives
4. Stories Running Within
5. Metaphors in Nature
6. Images Like Postcards
7. Still Awake in the Now
8. Transfiguring Faces
9. Chasing Ghosts Away
10. Benevolent Chaos

Where There Are Sparks DECEMBER 23, 24 / 2020

I thought I wasn't afraid to smile.
That songs didn't need to come out.
I thought that memories didn't need
To walk down a lane.
When the world is white and cold,
We listen, we pause,
Wonder about getting old, will we matter …

>I want to believe in moonlight, resting and dormant,
>With brightness renewed.
>I want to believe that God is a sphere,
>Whose center is everywhere, confined nowhere.

What do children
See when they look at trees and paint,
When they touch things not real?
We hope they still find truth.
Time constricts and flatters,
Childhood thoughts on holidays.
Are our stories true or just
What we dreamed they say?

>Lines are easy, curves take time,
>Embedding our nails with the peel of the moment,
>Glimmering gems that vein the mundane.

We watch the children of now,
Their heat flowing, like molten rock,
In a virtual world,
Where sparks can make a change.

Other Openings

Something sticks, and you don't know why
Something matters, but it's hard to hold
Being in a tower, removes you from ground
A chimney, from space,
A cloud, from form

> Sun streams in the kitchen window
> Trees a lattice for the light
> Birds are hungry, squirrels come
> Rustling leave under the feeder,
> The silence is deep and serene.

> A spiral means, there is no end
> A spiral makes room for adaptation
> Always looking for other openings
> We're almost out of the woods
> But not yet free, there's only wait and see.

> You hear the clanging of the gate,
> Unlocked door, open in the wind
> As though some ghosts were visiting
> In a moment of restoration,
> Like being in a boat at night.

Art transforms, evoking emotions
From ourselves, our transient notions,
Running on a track, train coming faster than you can run.
Lightening in a bottle, so many elements to catch.

> We study what has been forgotten,
> The constant gaps between things
> Where a presence out of place
> Is a mystery that's been missed,
> A miracle, if you can see it.

WE'VE ALL THOUGHT ABOUT GOING BACK IN TIME, OR IF SOMETHING NEVER HAPPENED. WHAT WE GET FROM THAT IS HOPEFULLY, SOMETHING THAT MATTERS ...

Unled Lives 〜⌒〜 JANUARY 16-17 / 2021

Lives unled, for all sorts of … reasons.
We make choices, events force our … hands.
But most of all, we're just human,
Becoming more, with time.

> While growth realizes, it narrows.
> Plural possibilities end.
> It's a strange sort of loss,
> We value who we are,
> While lamenting who we haven't become.
> Unreal lives can be forgotten,
> When we're swept up in our real ones.
> But sometimes we're confronted,
> And they shape us with meaning,
> Found in what never happened.
> History happening can engender
> Other lives we see
> Opening out to one side
> Like an exit that, viewed from outside
> Doesn't reflect our being. [Chorus]

Unled lives are real
To the extent we've imagined them
Every story has a turning point
For us to remember, for us to wrestle with

> Unlived lives can liberate
> Connecting the fragments within
> Connecting us to others, like and unlike ourselves,
> And though I value them,
> I don't wish to have led one.

SOMETIMES STORIES INSIDE OF US KEEP GOING ROUND AND ROUND ...
IF WE LET THEM ... MAYBE IT'S GOOD ... SOMETIMES, MAYBE NOT ...

Stories Running Within

Pieces of early sun, glancing off the lake's black gloss
Fringed by last night's snow
Rhythmic footsteps on the slippery pavement.
Glittering ice on the skeletal trees
Gray sky swaths overlap with the clouds
Day beginning as stories unwind.

> There's a wild history unsung
> People from the past, talking in your dreams
> People whose connection makes no sense
> But exist, strong as ever
> In a past that seeps and stains instead of fading,
> If you let it.

When you know someone well, you know them by their presence in space
At the edge of your vision,
In motion, in darkness, not just their face.
When we first meet people, we know them as they are,
But with time we see, the aura of possibility,
Heartbreak and beauty at once.

> Stories serve a purpose,
> Provoke thoughts that bind us to our lives
> Suggest we should be grateful,
> Sink deeper into the life we have, rather than
> Dreaming of what we don't.

We all dwell in the here and now, but always changing and new,
Our selves and lives refusing to stay, while we seek to define their meaning,
Which will always exceed what we can know or say.

Metaphors in Nature ⤳ JANUARY 31 / 2021

What is glamorous, teaches ambition
What is eccentric, teaches wit
What is passionate, teaches devotion …
When the cold is past and gone,
Rain so fine only a tingle on the skin
(A) bird caught in the house leaves a blessing,
Bringing the wind within.

Denial by a listener inflicts a blow
When there's no belief, a part can't survive
The work of telling is not enough
There's a danger we'll remain unchanged.

But trees stir in the darkness, listening
Birds make startled sounds when the stars are gone,
Some people you seem to know when you first see them,
Others you can spend your life with and not really know.

We are brave and wild, more life in us than we can bear
Fire inside us unfolding, to share …
Existence is miraculous, the world could be revoked,
Yet, it's instead, sustained …

We see metaphors in nature
Like no fear of what's coming,
Going with each moment, like nature does
A crisis reframes your vision.

PHOTO BY KEN BERNSTEIN

Images Like Postcards 〜〜〜

A way of holding, the world so loosely
Words get up and drift away.
But we remain, it's all within reach
At the mercy of our thoughts.

Leave off the lights, let things put on
Their daytime colors …
Shed the glaze the dawn slides
Across it all.

      These are images, we keep as postcards,
      From our lives
      From a world we did not fashion,
      But tries to fashion us.

Now I can see, snow in the green,
Unmelted in the hedge.
Dollops on branches, morph into shapes
Where the sparrows still sing.

      What are those mental pictures, shimmering at the edges
      Like trees leading perfect lives
      Together and alone … all at once
      Rooted but holding things loosely …

Spring can be slow, unfolding its power
Longer hours of rays
Begging us, to awake
See every day in color …

Still Awake in the Now

What would you do, with your last day?
In a last message, what would you say?

Plants glow, a still livid white
As if blasted by the moon shining down
Shadows too long, so dark and crisp
That they look, to be slashed.
>   That we notice and inhabit those places
>   Transforms us every day
>   In little ways, when we don't even know it
>   We're awake in the now, still awake in the now, awake in the now.
Flakes when they fall, fall to the side
Disrupted by wind, leave an uneven coating
We want to hold, that pure imperfection
Before it melts, through our fingers.

Are we just cameras, panning backwards
Into scenes we can't get back?
We know there's a reason to remember,
Even if we dare not, look directly.
>   What would you do, with your last day?
>   In a last message, what would you say?
>   You hear who you are in how you answer,
>   Whom you're becoming, whom you decline to be.
We mentally record what's around us,
Scents of cedar, and of pine,
Colors that appear, breeze on chimes,
A composite to hold, in the here and now.

PHOTO BY KEN BERNSTEIN

Transfiguring Faces 〰️ MARCH 1 / 2021

When you regain yourself, show who you are,
The person that God always sees,
Someone with authenticity,
Inner peace, lying in reach.

> We sit inside, sun-lacquered buildings
> Grass breaking through outside
> We watch and hear, but need to listen better
> To what's true for the person saying it.

> Light slants through the foyer's white space
> Tones a backdrop to the criss cross trees
> If we don't remember to turn ourselves outward
> We can forget that we must love as a need.

> When you watch a child grow and grow,
> It's pure consciousness coming into being
> Beautiful, complex and inexhaustible,
> How language comes and memories see.

Treasure the day, when you can glimpse that radiance,
Everyone we encounter, can have a transfigured face.
Cherish the moment, when you can feel the radiance,
Everything that you can see, in a transfigured face.

> We all have souls, that magic place within
> Ourselves that yearns, to be accepted.
> To have our truths heard is grace, after all
> The best way to acceptance, is to give it.

PHOTO BY KEN BERNSTEIN

Chasing Ghosts Away MARCH 13-15 / 2021

A ghost is not a thing in itself
Rather, it's a symbol for a need.
The most important part of its presence
Is the need that creates it.

> Sometimes a ghost is for your own comfort
> Loneliness creates the feeling of haunting,
> Laughter in the middle of sadness,
> A sunny day that's gray.

> We look at paintings, specific things
> In certain places, as ourselves, alone,
> Yet sensing spirits from other times
> That we look to others to confirm.

> Works may be old, but our experience is not,
> Renewing faith in the powers of art.
> But we can't forget that our needs have names,
> Spiritual stakes in a timeless game.

When you hear a song, I hope you see yourself, not the singer,
As your tapping the depths, immersed to your fingers.
When you attend to the words, I hope they're almost familiar,
Part of you but new, as our lives are far from linear.

> That's why stories are so important,
> Grabbing us by the imagination,
> Transporting us past long held beliefs,
> They can chase our ghosts away.

PHOTO BY LEAH SALOW

Benevolent Chaos

When is chaos, something good?
When does it bring, something new?
That's safe to embrace, rather than fear
Better to hold, than collecting tears.

      What can I hold onto?
      When things are spinning?
      Not worn toys from childhood,
      They're what I used to be, faded charms behind me.

Outside lies the languid glow
Of the unfrozen pond
Orange as a foil for the shadows
As the sun rises, gilding the still bare trees.

Inside live pictures in our minds
Telling us how to arrange our words
Then there's the negative space
That's also part of the portrait, part of what's seen.

      Do we want our hurt acknowledged?
      By someone who's been hurt
      The posture of forgiveness, can lead to palingenesis,
      Keep us from the mortality of lonely narcissists.

Chaos can be creative
Unveiling mysteries far greater
Mending tattered friendships
So there's space for peace, and maybe enlarging our hearts.

III. Capturing the Glow

These songs are about going after beauty so that it's a part of our space. Sometimes grace, kismet, luck, etc. causes us to be hit upside the head with it. Some say to wait for it. In a sometimes dystopian world, though, maybe we should make a better effort to seek and chase it, like it's a priority.

1. Future's Home Revisited
2. Capture the Glow
3. Adjusting Memory Lane
4. Headwind of Life
5. Living Like a Long Song
6. Gestures
7. Channeling Fenrir
8. Good Games
9. Growing Stories
10. Inside and Out

Future's Home Revisited ◌◌◌

MARCH 29 / 2021
& APRIL 2 / 2021
*prev. 2010

Holding someone, in your arms
Can be more natural, than a heartbeat.
I can learn too, what is plain to a child …
That life is simply, the sum of many lives …
Each lived one day at a time.

    (So) breathe each moment, feel your heart beat
    Take each day, like your own,
    Exhale your memories, into sunshine,
    You're present and past, future's home.

To cherish you, beautiful in life
You have something, inside of you,
Kind and strong,
God must be with you.
    You see something beautiful in a child
    And you almost live for it, feel like you'd die for it
    But it's not, yours to keep
    Every child is their own.

The tide can touch me, grasping out to the sand
Ever farther it takes me …
Crushed by blue,
I am yet returned to the shore … Returned to the shore

*I originally wrote this song in 2010, when my daughter and her twin were born, found it in 2021, and revised it by adding a bridge and a different, less frantic tempo, reflecting, perhaps, some wisdom gained since then, and possibly, being more relaxed with age. The twins have humored and supported me in this endeavor by taking and contributing many of the photos.

Capture the Glow ∿⌒ MARCH 27-29 / 2021

Lifting things, kept in a drawer,
Left unmolested by memory.
They are the same, but we who hold them
Are different now. Not resuming, just re-beginning.

Elements of craft and decoration,
Bright, floral accents.
Ambrosial color, human will to beauty as routine,
A story remembered, Catching up to ourselves.

      I want to capture that glow,

      A casting off of self.

      I want to feel that generosity.

      When love is like grace, worthiness

      Isn't what matters, what matters.

Tales and tides, come along
Not to extract but support.
When the embrace doesn't feel forged,
The effect is immersion, lacking in artifice, redeemed from mistakes.

      Sometimes we feel, we should have more than nature gives us.

      But the soul finds its own home.

      Sometimes we think, things should be otherwise.

      But our souls move on their own.

The objects are there, tracing our steps, purpose in our lives.
How we see and deal with death,
What is compassion?
Human life matters, destitution brings grace.

PAINTING BY LEAH SALOW

Adjusting Memory Lane

What we keep, or discard, builds another picture …
When we repave memory lane, we adjust our selves
The process of sifting through our photos,
Styles our emotions.
What we keep, or discard, builds another picture.

    In the past, we photographed, physical things to remember
    People, places, parts of us,
    Now we capture to engender.

What kinds of things do we need, for our future selves?
Numbers to call, a promise we made,
Artistry put on the shelf.

    There are photos to document, journalists going to the margins,
    Making a difference, for those written off,
    So that that can stop.

People cherish others, if they're cherished themselves,
No drama, only an encounter,
In strange places, and not where we expect
Something we see but don't account for.

    So when these pictures, are together, what should be left out?
    Not the people, bringing their places,
    We can be touched by their faces.

PYROGRAPH BY ERIC KAIN HUMPHREYS

Headwind of Life *APRIL 17-18 / 2021*

Shimmering trees, alive with birds,
Creak of the screen door, before the sun.
Released rain drops, flying up,
Brilliant in light on a pindo palm.

> Inverted foliage, reflected in the water,
> Gazing at ripples, upside down.
> Interrupted by a splash, falling twigs,
> Between branches, a frog makes a sound.

What is glory in a troubled world?
Thoughts like seeds, disappear in the ground.
There they lie, appearing to die,
But then they begin to grow.
Do they too, have a soul?

> Purplish smudges in the dimming evening sky,
> Light pools in the lake's dark moving ripples.
> Genres feel backward, created when they're done,
> Transient like wind toying with drops on a fixture.

In the headwind of life,
It takes self-will, maybe madness,
Take the leap anyway, put your name on it,
Because you have a vision, and it's worth the distance,
Worth the distance, to make a difference.

> It's the duality, of gazing outward and in,
> The harsh light of reality, and hazy glow of dream.
> There's a sense of questing, things can be unfixed,
> Twisting textures form into what they mean.

PAINTING BY ANDREW BOTTI

Living Like a Long Song

Living your life, like a long song,
Old and new, to revisit, in time.
Always a chance, to start again.
Apocalypse as an uncovering,
But not the end of days … not the end of days …

A story can change, when the light does.
What do we see in the shadows?
Are we awake, in another place?
A story with a different beginning …

Did we get turned around, lose our footing?
Miss the journey due to watching?
Is that another world, just behind us?
We see it from the corners of our eyes …

Doors open, lead to other doors,
Balancing the everyday that inspires,
The places that you build within, the places you step inside,
The places that are doors within, the places you reside.

We turn to look outside, see the sunset,
A collision of stains and color.
It's nothing we can match, when we create,
But moving and magnificent, it burns in us.

Gestures ∿ MAY 3-4 / 2021

Raining's a gesture, inviting the random.
Pouring and dripping, with a sense of wandering
Beneath the veneer.

Rendering landscapes, into abstraction,
Where images seep, with no surface,
Edgeless hues alongside.

No one knows where the time goes
It disappears all the same.
Like a staircase, standing alone
And moving through space,
Nothing really works out on its own,
The unexpected always comes home.

Colors like people, have values
Promising to live together, despite difference
Not discarded for lack of insistence.

Time can become space, stories and forms
In torrents that engulf you wherever you stand.
Therapeutic delirium, eye-catching and sublime,
Inherent qualities, only as assigned.

You get vertigo, from looking up and down,
Where a range of experience and emotion
Disguise how it all started with a gesture.

SCULPTURES BY ERIC KAIN HUMPHREYS

Channeling Fenrir ⟳⟿ MAY 7-9 / 2021

A fascination with Loki's son, but
You don't need to stick it to the man.
He's already left in a 'copter,
Not Odin, just an ugly Peter Pan.

I believe the world is round
Even if it doesn't feel that way.
Some fell off,
But the rest of us are here to stay.

Shape-shifting's got its benefits,
Wolves can wear sheep's clothing,
Pass as dogs, appearing docile,
Yet unable to be enclosed.

A force of nature can lie hidden,
But it cannot be tamed,
Awaiting time and circumstance
To realize its true name.

Do you have a Fenrir
Lurking somewhere within?
What alchemy would draw it out,
Cause its power to be unchained?

Good Games MAY 4 / 2021, MAY 10 - 12 / 2021

What makes good games is the commitment of the players
To the rules for invention.
It's not about capturing the king, but
Traveling the board, in style …

Soft buds green the bark
Nature's lace and fringe in bloom
Dark earth retains the sun,
Sucks the moisture down.

By the sea, the tide pools
Different life forms on display.
Colors and motion, all so staggering
Like being out in space.

Living things know the game, have internalized the rules,
They're not a reprieve
From the world,
But a chance to wrestle with its disputes.

Living things know the game, have internalized the rules.
Sometimes you should just play, not let your ego stop you.

These things say smart things
All so simply.
In a converging of obvious motifs
And complex motives.

PAINTINGS BY LEAH SALOW

Growing Stories ⟳ MAY 17-19 / 2021

There's a radio playing in your head, as you walk too close to the edge …
Change is what a story is, and we're an evolving place.
We store them in songs, pliable and living …
Music as different from recording, music aligned with song.

When you understand the seasons,
You know when to show up.
Because rocks are rocks, on which
We use our separate chisels.

You can greet the sea,
Restless on an overcast day,
Fluttering leaves on the salted shore,
Marine scent pervading.

Without sun glimmering through
You could miss the glittering
Coral, crushed sea glass,
Algae on a cave wall.

There's a radio playing in your head, as you walk too close to the edge …
Tunes winding with words heard and said,
lightsome takes on existential duress.

We grow stories like trees,
Something not there before,
Each word more than itself,
And everything a metaphor.

Inside and Out ⟿ MAY 24-27 / 2021

Does a year inside,
Change the way we hold our experience?
Are we revealed, not by fact,
But our contradictions, tended carefully?

Memories can be unfixed,
Transformed in recollecting, drifting on without end.
Beauty draws us, compels us to listen,
With its words, refracting like gems.

Fashion's been outside,
What it looks at and cannot see,
Defining what's desirable,
Mundane, and monstrous. Creating perceived needs.

Being caught inside,
Details glowed with meaning.
Everything related to everything else,
That curious confusion of inside and out.

We're seeking wholeness in a common kinship, fluency in a spiritual sense.
A certain nobility in being connected, tracking gratitude and resilience.

The outside's come back,
Birds competing with their songs,
Pollen in water like an oil slick,
Forest bathing where paths are long.

IV. Beginning to Imagine Better

ICS 6/2021 - 7/2021 • This past year, we have experienced world trauma in an unprecedented way. One hopes that we've learned something. As we re-emerge after months of lock-down, can we begin to imagine better? Not just for ourselves but the future of everyone? Do we see differently? These songs are about that.

1. Imagining Better
2. For the Near Future
3. When They Come
4. Igniting Words
5. Mustang Musings
6. Emergent Dancing
7. Mental Postcards Appearing
8. Souls' Integration
9. Through Others' Eyes
10. Threads of the Moment

PHOTO BY KATRINA WINZELER

Imagining Better ～⌒ JUNE 1-2 / 2021

A random Monday, at sunset. A day in a week, in time.
Sea lion surfacing, where you stand.
You go to grab your camera,
But orcas don't wait for those on land.

The air is charged and entrancing. Enchanted and inviting.
You settle for a genial seal,
No white eye patch and knowing,
Pinniped empathy revealed.

We can marvel at time's relativity,
Dancing above or outside of experience.
A lens to view things from beneath the surface,
Like the sun we can't stare at, yet attempt.

Present in the summer air. Present in the warm breeze,
Leaves flash against the sky,
Essence infusing as you inhale,
Fragrant tree trunks, skin, aligned.

Were we shockingly unclothed, without the complacency
of ordinary life? What do we now see?
Were we able to find, something else inside?
Something more to take with us, now that we're outside?

We have the power to imagine better, the potential to behold,
Tuck the year's events inside,
Holding them close, as we newly prize,
Drops falling through gaps in the canopy.

For the Near Future

Packing's part of us, like sorting through photos.
It's a narrative theory of self, building and re-building
By retelling our past, in what we take or leave,
From place to place.

We color things as more or less relevant with time,
Why do I keep that sweater?
Who was I at that concert with?
I should let go of that anklet.

The telling always comes, after the fact.
Sometimes ironic, sometimes detached.
Sometimes with new clarity, a phrase swapped out,
Recapturing a moment, and how it really felt.

Letters and photos are just paper,
without the memories we project onto them.
They capture a moment, maybe an expression,
but how do they make us feel?

So what have we gathered,
For this time and place?
What fits in the bag, whether by accident, subconscious or planned,
Comes with us to the near future.

SCULPTURES BY ERIC KAIN HUMPHREYS

When They Come JUNE 11-15 / 2021

A picture can be, an intense and casual surface,
A wall to walk through
For the subject souls to seek ours, catch us off guard,
Curiosity put into perspective.

It's like they're watching rather than looking,
For some secret, just out of sight,
Illuminating dark with silver, visionary creation
And unpredictable humor.

We want to converse, with the language of empathy,
Meet everything as a whole,
Art as evidence for what the world can be
From various directions.

Exposed to light, the strokes a filmy coating,
Froth on a whirlpool
To enter a surreal, imaginary palace, floating over
Pools on the floor in silence.

We view chance as a sidekick. Share in the shock as it becomes known.
Revelation on fast forward, contemplation art's goal. Art's goal.

So much of power's the ability to see
How willing others are to let you breath.
Faded color awaits, a new sun,
Ready when the ideas come.

PHOTO BY DEIRDRE SANDERS

Igniting Words

Words from the dead, left behind, don't change.
But for the living, language mutates over time.
Physical and sonic, in form and content,
When you take things, make them something else,
You've given them life, and they continue, even if discarded.

Green water, early sun, worn slanted stone walls.
When streets are chasms of light and shade,
You can sense spaces
That can hold you safely.

Outside the cityscape, lances of light stand tall
Coming through tree trunks, moss and earth.
You can feel the presence
Of vitality pervading.

You want to be real with people, whether just a few moments or a lifetime.
Words can do that, forge a connection, if you let them.

In your own castle, birdsong alights your ears,
Drifting through windows that let in sky.
You can hold the notes
That ignite new words.

PHOTO BY LEAH SALOW

Mustang Musings ⟜⟞

They're feral and ravishing,
Beguiling and strong.
Forebears swam from shipwrecks,
To the Crystal Coast, Shackleford Banks.

Run, run, run and run
Across the dunes of sand.
Splash, splash, splash and splash
Through the water and grass.
Wind in manes, graceful churning,
Moving so freely, creating yearning …

How can we seek them?
Only from a distance.
They've flourished on islands hundreds of years,
Survivors of failed settlements.

Stallions stir our imaginations,
Take us away from ourselves.
We ride alongside them in our minds,
Reach places we'd never find.

What do they give us,
With a winsome head toss?
A mental imprint of magnificence,
Images for fresh dreams.

PHOTO BY KATRINA WINZELER

Emergent Dancing ∽ JULY 2-4 / 2021

Tell me, is emergence a stronger force … than entropy?
We seem to favor it … emotionally.
We are sad for things shut down, root for things opening up.
Not a closed iris, but an explosion,
Flowers in time lapse video.

We were searching for how to find,
A sense of freedom and joy, in the smallest of spaces.
Now we see the beach again, as the tidal wave's pulled back.
What's survived? What didn't?

We're returning to common spaces.
Masks like dead bats on the sidewalk, we're sharing air with strangers,
In what we call culture, we go through the motions like victims of trauma,
Remembering how to dance.

Life changes, but we remain.
Stories get left behind, their subjects go on living
Words transmute, keep evolving.

We did not change our lives,
But the hope persists, redefining our space can remake our essence.
We may yet make peace, with the mortifying sense of porousness,
Transparency in our dreams.

PAINTING BY LEAH SALOW

Mental Postcards Appearing

Envision yourself, chest high in the ocean.
A sea lion swims across your path.
You hit the water, with your hands.
She turns and passes, splashing you back.

It's just a few minutes in a lifetime,
Hazy and gorgeous, a vivid instance,
The color of the sky on that day,
Drops in motion, like liquid chords.

It makes you wonder, why we try to control
Dissonance, where sight meets sound.
Perceiving all at once, conflates surface and depth,
As our central pitch keeps shifting.

We are stunned, by the physical world,
In relation to ourselves, or our souls.
Some artists notate, rather than produce,
Observed reality, to challenge us.

Experiences are seeing and feeling, thingness and thereness incarnate,
Magnetized, in technicolor, our mental postcards appearing.

Unquenchable interest in the visible world
Should immunize us to boredom.
Responding to things makes us fearless of error.
We can't help seeing, (and) they can't help but be.

Souls' Integration JULY 16-17 / 2021

There's a flame in the eyes,
Constant wakefulness, intensity.
When what's inside your head,
Transcends hesitation, emerging on a page.

When we're open, ready,
Ideas can express themselves,
With our hands, so directly,
Deliberation cannot interfere.

In carving the wood of our lives,
Fingers on the vertical grain,
There's a cohesion beyond what's within,
Unity in variety, the outward coming in.

Oppositional tones and moods
Arise within the same phrases.
Moving from scale to scale,
Polymodal harmony, emoting from the sounds.

Pieces can appear, savagely sincere.
In ways of looking in, how, bit by bit, things reflect our regard.

An edge is not where the paint stops,
Just where it changes color.
Each detail conveys, the artist's direct gaze,
Part of our souls' integration.

Through Others' Eyes ⟨⟩ JULY 21-22 / 2021

The library wasn't yet open,
But you encounter someone,
Who takes you to one that is,
Talking along the way.

He's not so different,
From the same neighborhood,
Could have even played as kids,
Crossed paths before.

Togetherness offers an odd revelation,
How and where to share pride, in the strangeness of selves.
It's easy to get caught up, in our own orbit,
Forget the identities that dwell.

Reminiscing about landmarks,
You exchange stories and a coffee,
It occurs to you that this contact,
Means more than what you see.

Understanding is being in the room, not just looking in the window,
It's more important than big ideas, or even shared goals.

We change each other,
As we move through space,
Meeting and accepting our paths' peculiarities,
As seen through others' eyes.

PHOTO BY KEN BERNSTEIN (1948-2021). LIKE THE MANY OTHERS WHOM HE TOUCHED, I MISS MY NEIGHBOR, FRIEND & TALENTED PHOTOGRAPHER, KEN BERNSTEIN, WHO PASSED AWAY IN LATE MAY. HIS MEMORY LIVES ON THROUGH HIS PHOTOS.

Threads of the Moment \sim\!\!\!\!\curvearrowright JULY 26-29 / 2021

Some memories are like a mirage,
Time still there, but not.
Extant in our minds but lost in the past.
What was it like when we were there?

We observe and try to act with kindness,
Without knowing what will happen.
Because not knowing doesn't justify
Not doing, seeing with no outcome.

With age, can we hope to grasp,
The peace of our future, present and past,
Woven together in a single thread,
Existing in each moment, if only we can own it … if only we can own it.

We are secretly entranced,
More than any triumphant fantasy,
By those dreams that escape or ruin,
Tainting the air with melancholy.

Can we really make decisions, as if all times were now,
Envisioning the future to choose wisely, in things big or small?

We begin in a non-verbal state of mind,
Studying how it's done,
To inhabit the drawings before us,
Tangles of line and color.

v. Following by Listening

8/2021-10/2021 • Sometimes I feel like creating is following by listening – no control, except to tweak and change things that sound off. Musical progressions that gel or come together, cause things that I have written about in journals I've kept for years, to become songs, sometimes combined with more current thoughts or environmental stimuli. I have observations, reactions to art or reading that are there and music brings them to life with editing caused by the notes, placement, playing them in a different order. These often include ideas, words, philosophical meanderings I hadn't at all envisioned being in any song. Sometimes I drop some words out because they don't work with the rhythm, and then realize I actually meant to say something else that is now emerging, maybe now as a different line …

1. Frequency Is Everything
2. Spell of Winding Down
3. Deconstruction Machine
4. Jewels in the Psyche
5. Many Layers
6. Hidden Beach
7. Giving It Play
8. Immersion
9. Subjects That Can Last
10. Sprung Rhythm

Frequency Is Everything ⟿ AUGUST 2-5 / 2021

It's like I am following, based on listening,
Exerting no control except to mold,
Things that sound off, and allow
The unexpected to come out.

We enjoy suspenseful conflict,
Between intention and actuality,
Merging inner and outer journeys,
Weather swirling in the psyche.

Frequency is everything,
Tuning in, mental switch on.
When you're awake and alive,
Together with others, as one.

We seek the wilderness sometimes,
For the state of mind, as sign
Radiant and exhilarating, that elsewhere,
We feel, is hard to find.

We are not solitary, no snow leopards are we,
But parts of a community, connected despite what we may choose to see.

It's living in anticipation,
Moving both slowly and chaotically.
It's just as clear what will happen,
As when it will be.

Spell of Winding Down

How do you capture, a quarrel in a song?
Are the words important? Or is it more, the emotional context?
And what is that closure, for which we long?
What is that closure, for which we long?

Patience, we know, is a virtue,
Especially with yourself and another.
An inward restraint, not acting like a rock,
But how you treat others.

It requires humility,
Putting aside your own needs,
Listening and working towards given ends,
Despite all the setbacks we see.

Narration can sometimes serve
As a deconstruction machine,
Helping us to figure out, puzzling interactions,
That could take us apart at the seams.

With stomps, strides and storms, can we channel the exuberance,
To swerve or sway, rather than beat against.

A musical altercation,
Gives operatic order to a line,
That sears rumbling timpani,
Before the spell of winding down.

METAL ART BY ERIC KAIN HUMPHREYS

Deconstruction Machine ⟿

When we're trying to rebuild,
Must things be taken down?
Not so much destroyed, but maybe defaced.
Maybe taken to another place?

Subjects are sometimes faceless,
To focus us, on what's bestowed on the world.
Whether or not it's good,
May yet unfold.

What's the value of a skull?
Currency in bare bone,
The value of farce to see one's soul,
Truth in metal, shown.

Imagination and innovation create powerful pictures.
Whether they remain, depends on our structures.
Thoughtfulness and humor, give rise to change in temperature.
Whether that breathes new life, lies in who we are to one another.

Changing features on a face,
Can shift the collective gaze.
Bringing hope with what's strange, that something new
Emerges from a parched land.

Jewels in the Psyche ⌇⌇⌇

A day like a fresh-cut peony,
Ocean aura, bright sun of capacity,
Air so clean and salty sweet,
How much of the present is yours to keep?

Light through the panes in the white turret,
Creating bright triangles on the wooden floor.
A nearby tree brushes the glass,
A wasp from the eaves by the door, as you leave.

Running along the shore path,
Low rock wall between you and the sea,
Liquid illuminations fall and rise,
Mirrors reflecting an opal sky.

People move along the path,
With dogs and carriages, turned to the waves,
Some breach the wall, climb wet rocks,
Meet winged accents, waterfalls.

Seagulls circle endlessly, clouds in seductive shades of ivory.
The moment immerses like an eternity, not an object, more an allegory.
Oh, if jewels could be memories.

Glittering gold lines the receding tide,
Brings you down to the beach.
Ankles in eddies, silver jetting fish,
Senses open, drinking in deep.

PAINTING BY LEAH SALOW

Many Layers ∿⌒ SEPTEMBER 5-7 / 2021

Do we all have infinite selves?
Everyone may remember you differently.
Depends on, how you wish to remember.
Dark corners lurk that aren't legible, so how do you know a soul?

Language speaks in many layers
As a path to getting to know someone.
If we're listening, we sense the vibes
From the worlds where others reside,
To find the doors that let us in.

There are so many archetypes,
Roles either taken or foisted upon us.
Even things simple can be made complex,
An everlasting web of intricacy, whether or not conscious.

Some say our minds are less entropic as we age,
That we experience less novelty.
Is it a question of muses trapped in amber?
Or just looking and forgetting to see?

Words can lead us to see through postures.
Protective armor, hiding in humor
Really can't cover for a moving experience,
Seeing a vision of what's to come, through what's come before.

Hidden Beach ～⌒ AUGUST 28-30 / 2021

Have you ever, been to a place
So timelessly here and now,
That it replaces your mind
With what you've just found?

There's a hidden beach that's invisible,
Until you step from the parking lot.
Onto the sand, it takes you away,
A warp in time and space.

The sound of singing wind and smell of rain,
Behind veiled clouds, lighted and gray.
Waves roll in slowly, and with each step,
Feet sink into dunes there laid.

It's almost prehistoric, dangerous,
You can feel the earth being reborn.
Crashing surf blends with the call of gulls,
Salt spray and foam on the stones.

Nature's a relentless painter, of dreams and poetic past.
Our characters can change, or maybe they're simply recast.

Deserted, but for a lone walker,
And something ominous at water's edge.
In time, the storms will pick up again,
When the ocean returns for the land.

PHOTO BY KATRINA WINZELER

Giving It Play ∿⌒

So many pelicans, on Stinson Beach,
There's one on the surface.
A porpoise duo erupts under it,
Throws it up, spooked and comedic.

There's a feeling of presence and absence all at once,
Like you're exercising force in your own space.
Pushing the edges, creating vectors,
The longer you look, the more you displace … displace.

You want to invent your own characters,
A narrative and a world,
Where they can function together.
All this exists, just right here, a treasure.

Breeze envelops like a blanket,
Undulating waves in the sun.
Life at foot speed is slow enough,
To include what chances to come along.

There's a skill in avoiding the same old pattern, a willingness to shift.
When we align with the truth of who we are, all things can fit.

Sometimes a change of plans,
Makes way for something unsought.
Even if the goal is unclear,
Giving it play can be worth a lot.

PAINTING BY LEAH SALOW

Immersion ⟨⟨⟿ SEPTEMBER 25-27 / 2021

When you jump in, you're in direct contact,
With not just the river, but underwater sludge.
Aspect serene yet churning, and coursing,
Headed somewhere, taking what comes.

In black light, disappearing dusk,
The sky's a bruised rose.
Fighting forecasts, inside and out,
Earth comes from below.

By diving in, we disrupt a pattern,
Where light and dark meet,
Bring life through abstraction,
Wetness and clarity.

Mercy, like love, is reflected to others once shown.
Florid incoherence washed and honed.
 Restoration values what we keep facing forward,
Memory the flip side of the coin, tossed on the swells of voyage.

By immersing, we improvise,
Go to another place
Where decisions aren't overthought,
And sleeping ideas awake.

PHOTO BY KATRINA WINZELER

Subjects That Can Last OCTOBER 1- 3 / 2021

You feel the eyes, a porcupine in the wild.
Ferociously elegant,
With sublime intelligence.
Her walk is subtle, yet fire.

Timbre and texture, unfold enigmatically.
Human desire is stronger than technology.
By focusing on details, we increase our grasp,
Of subjects that can last.

Then there's a glacier, ancient and powerful.
Surrounded by rain forest,
An exquisite mix,
Filled to the brim with beauty.

Collapsing connections into relevance can be dark,
But it's a space we can expand,
And create the world we want to start.

Water with icebergs,
Slate gray against the stark sky.
Crystalline pieces in the shimmer and flow,
Dancing a little off the ground.

PHOTO OF ST. THERESE MARKER IN ALASKA BY KATRINA WINZELER

Sprung Rhythm ⟋⟍ OCTOBER 8 -10 / 2021

On a shaky drive, one sunrise morning,
There's a shrine of St. Therese,
Off an isolated highway,
Built on a coast of blooming trees.

You open its memory door,
Walk through, thoughts coming
Like melted snow running in woods.
You see the view from within.

There's a sprung rhythm to wandering,
But the route can leave you dazed,
Like climbing an uneven staircase in a dream,
Illumination dispersing when you wake.

Part of the spell's the blurring of the line
Between indoors and outdoors,
Something sacred in the walls,
Speaking where the light falls.

Meandering can be a source of power,
starting with an angle, growing to flower.
You begin with something, see where it takes you.
Follow the rhythm, leaving meaning to find you. And it will. It will.

We learn who we are by living, and not before,
By doing, in practice, not theory remembered.
The tease of a view only draws us deeper.

Acknowledgements

Many thanks to Andrew Botti, Deirdre Sanders, Eric Kain Humphreys, Katrina Winzeler, Ken Bernstein (1948-2021), Leah Salow, my kids, Annika, Ari and Jake, and my husband, Josh, for your artistic contributions. These songs, whether posted for listening or in this book, would not be what they are without your inspiration and works. I am also grateful to my family for putting up with me and participating in as well as fostering creativity.

About the Author

Chiemi was born in Hawaii and lives with her family in Massachusetts. You can access recordings of her songs at https://chiemi1.bandcamp.com/ and https://soundcloud.com/user-377401109.

For more information about Chiemi, go to www.ChiemiMusic.com.